Little l

Mary anc

by Karen Williamson
Illustrated by Sarah Conner

CANDLE BOOKS

In the little village of Bethany there lived two sisters and their brother.

The sisters were called Mary and Martha.

Their brother was called Lazarus.

They were dear friends of Jesus.

He often had a meal with them...

or stayed as a guest in their home.

One day Jesus was journeying with his disciples when they came to Bethany.

"Please come and visit us!" said Martha.
So he did.

Mary was at home too.

When Jesus came into the house,
Mary immediately sat down with him.

Jesus talked and Mary listened carefully.

She wanted to hear the wonderful stories that Jesus told.

Martha had a lot to do in the kitchen.
She loved to cook.

Martha wanted to prepare a great meal for Jesus.

She was soon busy, chopping vegetables and boiling water.

After a while Martha thought,
"*Why doesn't Mary come and help me?*"

She began to feel quite cross.
So she went to Jesus.

"I'm doing *all* the work on my own," she complained. "*Please* tell Mary to help me!"

"Martha, you worry a lot about too many things," said Jesus.

"But sometimes you forget
what's really important."

"Mary has chosen the best thing to do," said Jesus.

"She has been listening to me.
I have been telling her about God's ways."

"Mary has taken my words into her heart," said Jesus. "*No one* can take that from her."